Worship ASAP

Other titles on special needs from Church House Publishing

Reflection Time: Developing a reflective approach to teaching and learning
Linda White

Raising the Standard, Flying the Flag: Challenging activities for all in RE at Key Stage 3
Janet Orchard

Connecting with RE: RE and faith development for children with autism and/or severe and complex learning disabilities
Liz O'Brien

Worship ASAP

40+ pick-up-and-use collective worship
ideas for special schools

Susan Murrell
Illustrations by Clare Parker

 CHURCH HOUSE
PUBLISHING

Church House Publishing
Church House
Great Smith Street
London SW1P 3NZ

ISBN 0 7151 4005 1

Published 2003 for the National Society (Church of England) for Promoting Religious Education
by Church House Publishing.

Copyright © The National Society (Church of England) for Promoting Religious Education 2003

Illustrations © Clare Parker 2003

Rebus and PCS symbols used with kind permission of Widgit Software Ltd Tel: 01926 885303.

Cover design by Church House Publishing

Printed in England by University Printing Press, Cambridge

Contents

Part 2   The worksheets

Appendix

Foreword

'I am come that they might have life and that they might have it more abundantly.'

John 10.10

In its guidance for inspectors and schools, 'Evaluating Educational Inclusion', OFSTED asks the question: 'Do the school's values embrace inclusion and does its practice promote it?' I can think of no more significant way in which a school, especially a Church school, can provide for its children than by seeking to enable everyone to participate in collective worship.

This publication both challenges and supports those providing religious education, worship and the nurturing of faith for children with a range of, often severe, educational needs. This inspirational book provides sound practical guidance which never underestimates the potential that *every* person has to learn and achieve. This book is thought-provoking and encouraging both to those serving in special schools and to those in mainstream schools.

The National Society established the Special Needs Fellowship to reflect its commitment to the development of religious education in all schools. The Council was particularly concerned to provide those working with these challenged children with an opportunity to share and develop the most effective practice.

We are all delighted that Susan Murrell's Fellowship has resulted in this innovative and very helpful publication.

Nick McKemey
Deputy General Secretary
The National Society and National School Improvement Officer
Church of England Education Division

Acknowledgements

I would like to thank the National Society for putting their trust in me, and for giving me the financial support to undertake this project.

I must also thank all at the Welsh National Centre for Religious Education in Bangor for their support and encouragement; I could not have completed this project without them. Particular thanks go to Mandy Robbins, Professor Leslie Francis, Dr Mike Fearn and Sam Jackson.

On a personal note, I would like to thank my family for their support and particularly my sister, Jan Whittington, who also proofread my work.

I very much appreciate the support of my colleagues at Ysgol y Graig: they gave me the inspiration and encouragement, and allowed me the time, to undertake this work.

This has been a wonderful time for me in my personal and professional development; thank you all.

Introduction

I am a practising teacher for children with SLD (severe learning difficulties), MLD (moderate learning difficulties), PMLD (profound and multiple learning difficulties), autism and challenging behaviour; I have worked at Ysgol y Graig (formerly Glan y Don) since September 1971. In April 1996 the Welsh counties went through a period of reorganization, which meant that an agreed syllabus had to be written for the new county of Conwy. I was invited to join the working party to represent special education, but, despite my involvement, much of the content was beyond the ability level of the pupils at my school. In 2000 I was successful in my application for a Farmington Institute Millennium Award, which enabled me to work on a link between the Conwy Agreed Syllabus and the ACCESS curriculum that we used in the school.

The staff at the school had agreed to develop the curriculum through six topic themes: Light, Myself, Homes, Celebrations, Living things, and Travel. Each topic is followed for a school term and is set at a level appropriate to the pupils in each class group. During my Farmington Institute Millennium Award year I was fortunate to be able to work at the Welsh National Centre for Religious Education in Bangor, where I had access to a wide range of books and publications. These resources gave me ideas and formed excellent background material, but very few were aimed specifically at our pupils who fall into the lower ability range.

By the end of my year I had produced material to support the teaching of RE at Ysgol y Graig and had organized a supply of archive boxes to cover the six major religions and the special occasions we cover within our topic themes. However, concerns were being raised among staff in relation to our weekly assembly. This is a time when pupils and staff are encouraged to gather together for a short assembly, which may or may not include an element of collective worship.

With this in mind I approached the National Society and was successful in gaining the 2001/02 Special Needs Fellowship, which would enable me to write this book of ideas for very simple acts of worship.

Background

At Ysgol y Graig we have 67 pupils on the roll, of whom 1 is a member of the Jehovah's Witnesses, 2 are Muslims and the rest are broadly Christian or of no faith. We organize collective worship in class groups, on a daily basis. We meet together as a whole school once a week for what we call 'assembly', which is really an act of worship of a 'broadly Christian' nature. In the past we have tried to split into junior and secondary assembly groups, but have gradually re-formed as a whole school because we find it works better for us. We realize it may seem inappropriate to keep together all ages from 3 to 19; yet most of the pupils do gain something, at their own level, from this joint worship. Some teachers find it quite daunting to have to stand up in front of the pupils and their many supporting staff to lead this important weekly act of worship with limited resources aimed at the pupils in the school. I felt that it would be useful if I could write a book of simple acts of worship that would stand alone: a book that could be picked up and used almost immediately because each act of worship would be a self-contained unit.

The research project

Special education is a term used to describe the education of pupils with a broad range of abilities. Many of our special schools cater for children with a variety of needs, ranging from SLD (severe learning difficulties) through MLD (moderate learning difficulties) and PMLD (profound and multiple learning difficulties) to autism and challenging behaviour. How can we offer meaningful worship both to the pupils in these schools and to special-needs children in mainstream schools?

The first question we must ask is: what do we mean by *worship*? My research took me to the Education Reform Act 1988 and then to the Religious Education and Collective Worship Circular number 1/94:

> 'Worship' is not defined in the legislation and in the absence of any such definition it should be taken to have its natural and normal meaning. That is, it must in some sense reflect something special or separate from ordinary school activities and it should be concerned with reverence or veneration paid to a divine being or power. However, worship in schools will necessarily be of a different character from worship amongst a group with beliefs in common.

Collective worship is a legal requirement. The Education Reform Act 1988 s. 6(1) states: 'All pupils in attendance at a maintained school shall on each day take part in an act of collective worship, subject to the right to withdraw.' Subsection (3) continues: 'The arrangements for the collective worship in a county or voluntary school required by this section shall be made – (a) in the case of a county school, by the headteacher after consultation with the governing body.'

Acts of worship can take place at any time during the school day, but must be on school premises. The school can decide whether there should be a single act of worship for all, or separate acts of worship for pupils in different age or school groups. Teachers and pupils may withdraw from collective worship. Acts of worship must be 'wholly or broadly of a Christian character'. If this is felt to be inappropriate for a particular school, the school can apply to its local SACRE (Standing Advisory Council on Religious Education) for this clause to be lifted.

The dictionary definition of *assembly* is 'a collection or company of persons brought together; a meeting; a congregation'. Assemblies in schools are often pupil-centred and may involve pupils as active participants. Assemblies should help to foster a sense of community within each school and should be a learning experience of real quality. A school assembly need not include any element of collective worship. Pupils and staff then need not be compelled to join in unwanted worship.

So what happens in our special schools? How appropriate is it to attempt to gather the pupils together? How easy is it to cope with wheelchairs, standers and other aids? How much pressure are we putting on pupils who cannot cope with noise and with large groups of people? How relevant to our pupils are collective worship and assembly?

When I first decided to write these short acts of worship I realized that I would need to do some research; I could not assume that every school had the same resources, or did the same things, as mine. My investigation was designed to find out what happens in collective worship and assemblies in other special-needs schools. At Ysgol y Graig we have the use of two sets of hymnbooks and songbooks, but do all special schools? At Ysgol y Graig we sing a number of different songs, yet tend to come back to a few favourites, but do all special schools? At Ysgol y Graig I lead the assemblies every alternate week, with the class teachers, in rota, leading in the other weeks, but what happens in other special schools? In order to find out how other schools undertook their assemblies, I sent out a questionnaire to the headteachers in 495 special schools in England.

At the beginning of the questionnaire I gave brief definitions. Assembly was defined as 'a gathering together, which may or may not include an act of collective worship'. Collective worship was defined as 'the daily act of worship'.

Worship in the special school – results from the survey

I was grateful to receive replies from 220 schools, representing a 44 per cent response rate; headteachers completed 59 per cent of the questionnaires. Of the 220 respondents, 37 per cent were male and 63 per cent were female; 77 per cent were between 40 and 54 years of age; and 83 per cent had been in teaching for more than 16 years. Special education was the main subject area of 35 per cent of the respondents when they trained. Less than half of the respondents (49 per cent) said they belonged to a church or religious group.

Respondents were asked which faith groups were represented by their pupils. The following faith groups were present: Christianity in 100 per cent of schools; Islam in 54 per cent; Hinduism in 36 per cent; Sikhism in 21 per cent; Judaism in 18 per cent; Buddhism in 8 per cent; Others (including Jehovah's Witnesses) in 9 per cent. With this information in mind, it was interesting to make a comparison with the percentages of schools having regular contact with faith groups or religious leaders: Christianity 77 per cent; Islam 18 per cent; Hinduism 10 per cent; Sikhism 10 per cent; Judaism 12 per cent; Buddhism 5 per cent; Others 2 per cent. It is clear that there is a discrepancy between the faith groups represented by the pupils and the contact the schools have with faith groups. Is this because we cannot get faith groups and religious leaders to come into the special schools, or because we have not invited them?

Who leads assembly?

Traditionally it was always the headteacher who led the school assembly, but do we follow this tradition in special schools? Of the schools that responded, 87 per cent said that headteachers led assembly; 81 per cent said teachers led assembly; 54 per cent have assembly led by class groups; and 41 per cent asked faith leaders to lead their assembly at least once every term. To reflect this information, this book has been written in such a way that either an individual or a class group could use it to lead an assembly.

Who leads collective worship?

Collective worship is defined as the daily act of worship; so who leads collective worship? Of the schools that responded, 74 per cent said the headteacher led collective worship; 73 per cent said teachers led collective worship; 31 per cent had collective worship led by class groups; and 41 per cent asked leaders of faith groups to lead their collective worship at least once every term. To reflect this information, this book has been written in such a way that either an individual or a class group could use it to lead collective worship.

Format of assembly

Assembly was held on a daily basis in 38 per cent of the schools that replied, with a further 23 per cent meeting twice a week. Of those responding, 17 per cent always followed a set pattern for assembly; 60 per cent usually did so; 11 per cent sometimes and 12 per cent never followed a set pattern. Of all the schools that replied to the questionnaire, only 2 per cent said that they never came together as a whole school for assembly.

Format of collective worship

According to the Education Reform Act 1988: 'All registered pupils attending a maintained school should take part in daily collective worship' (s. 6(1)); and 'It is the headteacher's duty to secure this' (s. 10(1)(a)). Yet, according to the data received, only 41 per cent of the schools said that each pupil participated in collective worship on a daily basis (with 9 per cent doing so four times a week; 9 per cent three times a week; 13 per cent twice a week and 18 per cent once a week). The whole school came together once a week for collective worship in 26 per cent of those responding, while 14 per cent came together as a whole school every day. Only 10 per cent of respondents said their pupils met in class on a daily basis, with a further 19 per cent meeting once a week as a Key Stage group.

Content of assembly and collective worship

When the questionnaire asked if assembly had a religious input, 18 per cent said 'always'; 41 per cent 'usually'; 40 per cent 'sometimes'; and 1 per cent 'no'. Assemblies usually followed a set pattern in more than 76 per cent of the schools. Prayers were said as part of the assembly in over 85 per cent: of these, 24 per cent reported they had their own school prayer; 17 per cent said the Lord's Prayer; 41 per cent took prayers from a book; and 48 per cent used prayers made up by staff and pupils.

Hymns were often sung as part of assembly in over 76 per cent of the schools. Religious songs could form part of assembly in almost 89 per cent, and non-religious songs were used in almost 78 per cent. Only 24 per cent used a hymnbook or songbook on a regular basis. Over 45 per cent of the schools said that their pupils preferred action songs; the song that was quoted most was 'He's got the whole wide world in his hands'.

Visual aids were employed by most of the schools, with 89 per cent making use of pictures; about 73 per cent using symbols; just under 68 per cent employing words; and just over 92 per cent props. Other visual aids included puppets, whiteboards, overhead projectors and the computer.

Assembly followed the school topic or theme in over 70 per cent of schools; and the theme of assembly was often continued, or followed up, in the classroom in over 87 per cent.

The content of collective worship was not explored in the questionnaire, although almost 80 per cent of those who responded felt that collective worship was of benefit to the children in their school. Over 80 per cent felt that collective worship was an important part of school life, and almost 71 per cent felt that it was enjoyed by most of the children in their school. Only 10 per cent felt that collective worship was not necessary. Over three-quarters (79 per cent) felt that collective worship helped pupils to adopt the school values. Over a third (37 per cent) felt that collective worship helped pupils to be nurtured by their own religion, while nearly a half (46 per cent) felt that it helped pupils to develop Christian beliefs.

Over 43 per cent of those responding felt that collective worship helped pupils to develop an interest in religion; almost 32 per cent felt that it helped pupils to develop a relationship with God. It was interesting that 69 per cent felt that collective worship helped pupils to be tolerant of other religions.

Perceived benefits

So why do we have collective worship in our special schools? We know that it is a legal requirement, but does it benefit our pupils and if so, how? Over 71 per cent of respondents feel that collective worship helps pupils to develop spiritually; over 78 per cent think that it helps pupils to distinguish between right and wrong; almost 85 per cent believe that it helps pupils to respect each other; and over 81 per cent consider that it helps pupils to develop socially. All of these are areas that our pupils find difficult; it is good to realize that collective worship can be another tool for us to use.

Faith leaders

It was interesting that the replies show that 71 per cent feel leaders of faith communities should be involved with collective worship in schools, and 61 per cent think that they should lead special services. The questionnaire demonstrates that teachers would like faith leaders to get involved in special schools; maybe they could take the initiative and invite them? The faith leaders in my area are only too pleased to take assemblies for our special occasions, and they try to come to school as often as they are invited. We have also been made very welcome at local churches on numerous occasions. The logistics of getting an entire school and its staff to church for a short service are not easy, but the benefit for the pupils is worth the effort. It is not easy to describe the beauty of a stained-glass window, or to tell of the depth of sound that an organ makes; these things need to be experienced at first hand.

The book

Guided by the information from the survey, I set about writing. The resulting book is divided into two parts: the first contains a series of short acts of worship. The second part consists of a matching series of simple worksheets, to continue the theme of the day's worship into class work.

Part 1

The acts of worship

Introducing the acts of worship

Worship at Ysgol y Graig

As I have said earlier, at Ysgol y Graig we get together once a week for whole-school worship, which we call 'assembly'. It is quite an undertaking to gather all the staff and children together in the hall. As in other special schools, many of our pupils are in standers, adapted seating or wheelchairs. It often takes ten minutes or more for everyone to arrive. Some of our pupils cannot cope with the noise or the confined space; they have the option of staying in their own classroom.

Many of our pupils follow the TEACCH (**T**reatment and **E**ducation of **A**utistic and **C**ommunication-handicapped **CH**ildren) method of work, and we felt it to be essential that this should be continued in assembly. We now have a portable box that contains everything needed for assembly: a cloth, a fragrant candle, matches (in a suitable container), and a set of symbols. We use 'Writing with Symbols 2000', and the box contains a laminated set of symbols, which denote: song, story, prayer, and golden frame awards. These symbols are displayed from left to right and act as an order of service. Each symbol is removed as that section of the worship is completed. This is a clear visual reminder for each pupil of what is happening, and how long they will have to stay in the hall for assembly. Our headteacher usually leads the golden frame awards, when all pupils who have achieved something special during the week have their pictures displayed in the golden frame. Our assembly ends when everyone joins in saying our school prayer:

> O God be with us through this day
> and help us to be good.
> Kind thoughts to think, kind words to say,
> to do the things we should.
> Amen

The fragrant candle is lit to indicate the start of assembly, and everyone helps to blow it out when assembly is 'finished'.

Worship in this book

When writing this book of worship ideas my aim was to produce something very simple; for which I make no apologies. I wanted resources that could be picked up and used, needing almost no preparation by the worship leader.

I have set out one act of worship on each page. Each includes a list of suggested items that can be used as props; three or four hymns or songs that fit into the theme (though at Ysgol y Graig we use only two in each service); a brief outline of the theme; and a short and simple prayer.

Each act of worship in this book can also be used as a starting point, if the person leading the worship would like to expand the idea further.

The following icons have been used to indicate the different sections:

     Resources needed

     Songs

     Outline of theme

     Prayer

Note on abbreviations

In the lists of songs, 'MP' indicates that the music can be found in *Mission Praise*; 'JP' denotes *Junior Praise*; and 'K' represents *Kidsource*. Further details of each of these songbooks are in the Bibliography.

Section 1 Light

- Christingle
- Advent
- Hanukkah
- Diwali
- Candles
- Creation
- Traffic lights
- Colours

Christingle

Needed

A Christingle: if possible, one per class or per pupil

Matches or lighter

Songs

'Give me oil in my lamp' – MP 167

'Lord, the light of your love' – MP 445

'Oh, sing about Christingle'

The Christingle Service is a tradition that was started in Scandinavia to remind Christians about Jesus.

Show the children the Christingle.

Talk about the things used to make it:

The orange represents the world.

The candle is Jesus, the light of the world.

The ribbon represents the love of Jesus, which goes around the world. (It is often red, to represent the blood of Christ.)

The cocktail sticks are the four seasons.

The fruit represents the fruits of the earth and the way that God feeds his people.

Light the candles on the Christingles as you sing a song.

Prayer

Thank you, God, for the four seasons of the year: for spring, summer, autumn and winter. Thank you for sending your light to spread around the world.

Amen

See worksheet for a picture to colour.

Advent

Needed

An Advent ring, with five candles

Matches or lighter

Songs

'Lord, the light of your love' – MP 445

'This little light of mine' – JP 258

'Away in a manger' – MP 47

The **Christian** festival of light is called 'Christmas'; it lasts for twelve days. There is a period of preparation for four weeks before Christmas; this is called 'Advent'. Some churches set up an Advent ring, which has candles in a circle of evergreen.

Show the children an Advent ring.

Talk about the four candles around the outside. Explain how people in a church will light one more of these on each of the four Sundays leading up to Christmas: one on the first, two on the second, and so on.

These four candles (which are usually red) represent:

- The people of God
- The prophets
- John the Baptist
- Mary

The fifth candle, in the centre, is there to represent Jesus Christ and is lit on Christmas morning. (This is usually white.)

Prayer

Thank you, God, for sending Jesus, who was born on Christmas Day.

Amen

See worksheet for a picture to draw and colour.

Hanukkah

Needed

A hanukiah and candles

Matches or lighter

Optional:

A dreidel game

Latkes (potato cakes) and doughnuts

(For latkes recipe, see Appendix.)

Songs

'Give me oil in my lamp' – MP 167

'He's got the whole wide world' – MP 225

'Shalom'

The **Jewish** festival of light is called 'Hanukkah'. It lasts for eight days and usually occurs in the month of December.

Every night the candles of the hanukiah are lit. It has eight branches, plus an extra (ninth) light called the 'servant light', which is used to light the others. One candle is lit on the first night, then two on the next, and so on. The candles burn for half an hour each night.

Hanukkah is a happy time, when children play the dreidel game, and people eat latkes and doughnuts. These foods are cooked in oil and so are reminders of the miracle of oil.

This happened a long time ago, when the land of the Jews had been taken over by foreigners. After they had driven the foreigners away, the Jewish people had only enough oil to light the temple lamp for one night, yet it was going to take over a week to fetch more. Miraculously, the lamp stayed alight for eight days. So, at Hanukkah the hanukiah is lit.

Light the candles and taste the foods.

Prayer

Thank you, God, for sending oil to keep us warm; to give us light; and to feed us.

Amen

See worksheet for a picture to colour.

Diwali

Needed

Diva lamps

Matches or lighter

The story of Rama and Sita

Coloured rangoli patterns

Decorated hand-shapes

Optional:

Sweets

(For the story of Rama and Sita, and a recipe for sweets, see Appendix.)

Songs

'Stand up, clap hands' – JP 225

'He's got the whole wide world' – MP 225

The rainbow song

The **Hindu** festival of light is called 'Diwali'. This is a family festival.

Homes are cleaned and decorated. Using coloured rice flour, women make rangoli patterns at the entrance to their homes to welcome Lakshmi, the goddess of wealth. Small clay lamps called 'divas' are lit everywhere. There are firework displays, and people enjoy special sweets.

Asian girls celebrate festivals by decorating their hands with mehndi patterns.

Light some diva lamps (or use night lights in small pots) while you tell the story of Rama and Sita.

Show the children some coloured rangoli patterns.

Show the children some decorated hand-shapes.

Share out some sweets (if you are using these).

Prayer

Thank you, God, for the colours that are around us in our world.
Thank you for making the world a special place for us to live.
Amen

See worksheet for a picture to colour.

Candles

Needed

A circular cloth

A variety of candles

Songs

'Who put the colours in the rainbow?' – JP 288

'This little light of mine'

'The Spirit lives to set us free' ('Walk in the light') – MP 664

Put the cloth on the floor in the centre. Arrange your benches and chairs in a large circle round it.

Place a variety of candles (unlit) on the cloth: for example,

baptismal; church; ornamental; emergency; birthday; tea-lights; and diva lamps.

Talk about the different candles and what they are used for.

Talk about people who have to use candles because they have no other light.

Find a birthday boy or girl, light some candles for them, and let them blow these out.

Prayer

Thank you, God, that we have candles that give us light. Thank you for sending your son Jesus to be a light to the world.

Amen

See worksheet for a picture to colour and match.

Creation

Needed

A 'Creation' storybook

or

Pictures of: day and night; earth and sky; land and sea; plants; sun, moon and stars; birds and fish; beasts and animals; man and woman.

Songs

'Who put the colours in the rainbow?' – JP 288

'Who made the twinkling stars?' – K 8

'I love the sun'

Read the 'Creation' book to the children, or look at all the pictures in turn.

Talk about what it would be like if the world was in darkness all the time.

Talk about how it would be if we had no water, no rivers and no seas.

Talk about how it would be if we had no animals, birds and fish.

Talk about how it would be if we had no people on the earth.

Prayer

Thank you, God, for making our world. Thank you for the animals, the birds and the fish. Thank you for food to eat and clothes to wear. Thank you for the sun and the moon. Thank you, God, for making everyone.

Amen

See worksheet for a picture to draw and colour.

Traffic lights

Needed

A circle each of red, amber and green paper

and/or

A picture of traffic lights

A torch with coloured filters

Songs

'Stand up, clap hands' – JP 225

'He's got the whole wide world' – MP 225

'If you're happy and you know it'

Sometimes we have to have rules. If your Mum or Dad tells you to stop doing something, you should listen.

When cars go along the road they have to obey the rules. There are lots of signs to tell drivers what they can do.

How many people have seen traffic lights?

The traffic lights are there to tell the cars and lorries when they have to stop and when they can go.

Look at the three colours and talk about stopping, getting ready and going.

Talk about pedestrian crossings and how important it is to wait for the green man before you walk across the road.

Prayer

Dear Lord, help us to obey the rules. Help us to stop when we are told. Help us to be ready and to go when we are told.

Amen

See worksheet for a picture of traffic lights to colour.

Colours

Needed

A piece of material or card for each of the colours of the rainbow

A piece each of black and white material

Songs

'Who put the colours in the rainbow?' – JP 288

The rainbow song

'He's got the whole wide world' – MP 225

Hold up a piece of material. Ask all who are wearing clothes in that colour to stand up, or to put their hands up.

Do this with each colour in turn.

Ask one child who represents each colour to come to the front. Then sing the rainbow song, using the children as a prompt.

Cover this group with the black material and ask the children to think what it would be like if everything was black. Do the same with the white material.

Prayer

Thank you, God, for giving us such lovely colours in our world. Thank you for giving us eyes to see the colours.

Amen

See worksheet for a rainbow picture to colour.

Section 2 Myself

- Hands
- People who help us
- Body parts
- Shoes
- Hats
- Myself
- Baptism

Hands

Needed

Your hands, some thick gloves and a wrapped sweet

Pictures of people using their hands to work

A picture of hands decorated with mehndi

Songs

'Jesus' hands were kind hands' – JP 134

The finger family

'Stand up, clap hands' – JP 225

Talk about hands and how we use them. Talk about all the things we do with our hands.

Look at the pictures of Hindu girls, who decorate their hands with mehndi when they are celebrating special days.

Talk about what it would be like if we didn't have hands. Think about the people in countries at war who have lost their hands because of bombs and land mines.

Get a child, or an adult, to put on the thick gloves and give them a simple task to perform, such as opening a sweet. Then let them try again without the gloves.

Prayer

Thank you for our hands. Help us to use our hands wisely to help other people.

Amen

See worksheet for a picture of hands to colour with patterns.

People who help us

Needed

Pictures of people who help us

The Teddy Horsley book *Neighbours*

A variety of hats or uniforms

Songs

'When I needed a neighbour' – JP 275

'He's got the whole wide world in his hands' – MP 225

The magic penny

Talk about people who help us at school.

Talk about people who help us at home.

Talk about people who help us in the community.

Look at the hats and uniforms and decide who would wear them.

Read the Teddy Horsley book *Neighbours* (in which Betsy Bear helps her neighbours).

Prayer

Thank you, God, for all the people who help us every day. Thank you for our Mums and Dads. Thank you for all the people who help us in school.

Amen

See worksheet for a matching game.

Body parts

Needed

Yourself and some pupils

Footprints or handprints

Songs

'Heads, shoulders, knees and toes'

'He gave me eyes so I could see' – JP 74

'He's got the whole wide world in his hands' – MP 225

Talk about your body and ask the children to name the body parts.

Look at the different colours of eyes.

Look at the different colours of hair.

Look at the different sizes of hands.

Look at the different sizes of feet.

Look at the difference in height between a young child and an older child.

Discuss the fact that although we are all different, we are all as important as one another.

Prayer

Thank you, God, for making us all. We are all different, but we know that in your eyes we are all special. Help us to work together to make our world a good place to live.

Amen

See worksheet for a picture to colour.

Shoes

Needed

A variety of footwear in a variety of sizes, e.g. wellington boots; trainers; shoes; Piedro boots; sandals; walking boots; slippers

Songs

'One more step along the world I go' – JP 188

'Oh, the grand old Duke of York'

'He's got the whole wide world in his hands' – MP 225

Look at each pair of shoes in turn.

Talk about the person who would wear the shoes.

Discuss the occasion when they would wear them.

Talk about the shoes being a 'pair', and that we need both shoes to make the pair.

Talk about how the shoes protect our feet.

Prayer

Thank you for shoes and boots to give support and protection to our feet. Thank you, God, for giving us support and protection as we walk on the path of life.

Amen

See worksheet for pictures to colour and match.

Hats

Needed

A variety of hats, e.g. sun hat; woollen hat; safety helmet; bicycle helmet; motorcycle helmet; bride's veil; policeman's helmet; nurse's cap; firefighter's helmet

Songs

'One more step along the world I go' – JP 188

The magic penny

'Heads, shoulders, knees and toes'

Look at each hat in turn.

Talk about the person who would wear the hat.

Discuss the occasion when they would wear it.

Talk about how some hats are needed to protect your head.

Talk about the hats that people who help us wear.

Prayer

Thank you for hats to give us protection for our heads. Thank you, God, for giving us support and protection as we walk on the path of life.

Amen

See worksheet for a picture to colour.

Myself

Needed

A shoebox, with a mirror glued inside, wrapped up or decorated so that it looks like a present.

Songs

The magic penny

'Stand up, clap hands' – JP 225

'He's got the whole wide world in his hands' – MP 225

Show the children the box and tell them that you have a very special present inside. Ask them to guess what is in the box.

You can give them clues:

- ■ 'This gift is unique.'
- ■ 'This gift is very special.'
- ■ 'There is only one of these in the whole world.'

Let a few of the children handle the box and try to guess what is inside.

Let a child open the box. When the child looks inside they will see themselves in the mirror. Ask the child, 'Tell everyone what you can see.'

Tell the child that he or she is very special, and that 'There is only one of you in the whole world.'

Prayer

Thank you, God, for making us all. Thank you for making us special.

Amen

See worksheet to draw a picture of yourself in the mirror.

Baptism

Needed

A doll baby, dressed for a baptism

A baptismal candle

Water

A cake to share

Songs

'Give me oil in my lamp' – JP 50

'Peace, I give to you' – MP 553

'He's got the whole wide world in his hands' – MP 225

Talk to the children about their names. Tell them that they were each given a name when they were born.

Christians take their babies to church to be baptized. Act out putting water on the head of the baby and giving the child his or her name.

Show the baptismal candle and tell the children that this is given to show that the baby has 'passed from darkness to light, and now belongs to the kingdom of God'.

Celebrate the baptism by sharing the cake. Explain to the children that families usually have a party to celebrate the baptism.

Prayer

Thank you, God, for our names that are special to us. Bless all babies and keep them safe as they grow up.

Amen

See worksheet for a picture to colour.

Section 3 Homes

- Homes
- Safety in the home
- The environment
- Furniture in the home
- Family life
- Jewish festival of Sukkot
- Animals and their homes
- Homeless

Homes

Needed

Pictures of different kinds of dwellings

A tray of sand, some wooden blocks and some water
(preferably in a watering can)

Songs

'The wise man built his house upon the rock' – JP 252

'God is good, God is great' – K 73

'He's got the whole wide world in his hands' – MP 225

Talk about the kinds of dwelling that the children live in.

Do they live in: a house; a flat; a bungalow; a farmhouse; or a caravan?

Tell them that some people who live in hot countries live in houses made of branches and mud.

Talk about the need to have a good foundation for their house.

Do an experiment using the wooden blocks. Build up some blocks on a firm surface and build up some other blocks on the sand. Then pour water over the two sets of blocks and watch the blocks on the sand fall.

Prayer

Dear God, help us to build strong foundations. Be with us so we can grow from strength to strength.

Amen

See worksheet for a picture to colour.

Safety in the home

Needed

Some pictures of dangerous items: knives, hammer, scissors, etc.

Some symbols that indicate 'not available'

Songs

'When I needed a neighbour' – JP 275

'All things bright and beautiful' – MP 23; JP 6

'Bind us together, Lord' – MP 54; JP 17

Talk about things in the home that can be dangerous.

Stress to the children that they must not use these things unless they are supervised.

Place one of the 'not available' symbols (a 'no entry' sign) on each pictured dangerous item.

Talk about being safe all the time and listening to what an adult says.

Prayer

Please, God, keep us safe all the time. Help us to be sensible and to listen to what an adult tells us.

Amen

See worksheet for a 'not available' sign to colour.

The environment

Needed

Some empty boxes and assorted rubbish

A dustbin

Some recycling bins clearly labelled for paper, glass and cans

Songs

'Thank you, Lord, for this fine day' – JP 232

'He's got the whole wide world in his hands' – MP 225

'Think of a world without any flowers' – JP 254

Talk about the world in which we live.

Talk about food and all the packaging. What happens to all the paper and cardboard?

Discuss ways we can help the environment by recycling.

Get the children to put items into the correct containers.

Talk to them about being careful not to drop litter.

Prayer

Help us to take care of the world in which we live. Help us to be more thoughtful about the precious resources.

Amen

See worksheet for a matching game.

Furniture in the home

Needed

The story of Goldilocks and the three bears

A chair, a table and a bed

Songs

'When Goldilocks went to the house of the bears'

'He gave me eyes so I could see' – JP 74

'The wise man built his house upon the rock' – JP 252

Talk about furniture that we have in the home.

Talk about which rooms you would put the furniture in.

Tell the story of Goldilocks and the three bears.

Try to act it out.

What happened to the baby bear's chair?

Get the children to name the items of furniture.

Prayer

Thank you, God, for giving us nice homes to live in. Thank you for all the things in our homes that make them special for us.

Amen

See worksheet for pictures to colour and match.

Family life

Needed

Teddy Horsley book *The Broken Leg*

Things for doing jobs around the house, e.g. duster and polish; tea towel and saucepans; cutlery

Songs

'When I needed a neighbour' – JP 275

'Stand up, clap hands' – JP 225

'He's got the whole wide world in his hands' – MP 225

Talk about jobs that need doing around the home.

Who does the dusting and polishing?

Who washes the pots and dries them up?

Who sets the table for a meal?

Who makes the bed?

Read the Teddy Horsley book *The Broken Leg*. (Teddy Horsley meets Jesus in all who help him.)

Prayer

Thank you, God, for people who help us in the home. Thank you for our Mums and Dads; thank you for our brothers and sisters. Help us to be helpful in the house.

Amen

See worksheet for a picture to colour.

Jewish festival of Sukkot

Needed

A shelter, or tent, made from a frame and some material

(If possible, hang some fruit from the roof.)

Songs

'All things bright and beautiful' – MP 23; JP 6

'He's got the whole wide world in his hands' – MP 225

'When I needed a neighbour' – JP 275

The Jewish Feast of the Tabernacles is celebrated in the autumn and could be used as an alternative to Harvest. The word 'Sukkot' comes from 'sukkah', the Hebrew word for 'hut'.

The festival recalls the time when the Jews were travelling through the desert from Egypt to the land of Israel, after escaping from the Egyptians. They made shelters, or huts, to live in.

At Sukkot Jews build their own sukkah outside and try to live in it for a week. The roof is made of branches and hung with fruit. They like to see the stars through the roof.

Try to imagine what it would be like to be homeless.

Where would you sleep?

How would you keep warm and dry?

Where would you cook your food?

Share some fruit with the group.

Prayer

Thank you, God, for giving us a home to live in and food to eat. Bless all the people who have no home, no family or no friends.

Amen

See worksheet for a picture to colour.

Animals and their homes

Needed

Pictures or models of animals

Pictures of: a farm; the jungle; a house

The story of Noah

Songs

'All things bright and beautiful' – MP 23; JP 6

'He's got the whole wide world in his hands' – MP 225

'Stand up, clap hands' – JP 225

'The animals went in two by two'

Talk about animals and where they live.

How many children have pets in their home?

Are there any pets in school?

Look at the animal models or pictures and have a matching game to decide where they might live.

Talk about animals that live underground.

Discuss the importance of protecting the habitat of animals and birds.

Tell the story of Noah.

Prayer

Thank you for all the animals in your kingdom. Help us to treat them kindly and with respect.

Amen

See worksheet for a matching game.

Homeless

Needed

Two blankets

or

A large cardboard box

Songs

'When I needed a neighbour' – JP 275

'Stand up, clap hands' – JP 225

'He's got the whole wide world in his hands' – MP 225

Ask the children where they live.

Talk about nice warm houses.

Tell them that some people do not have homes.

Choose some children to come to the front and ask them to pretend that they don't have a nice home to go to.

Give them a blanket or the cardboard box and talk to them about sleeping outside in the cold with only that to keep them warm.

Prayer

Thank you, God, for our nice homes. Thank you for our Mums and Dads who look after us. Please bless all the people who have not got a home and keep them safe.

Amen

See worksheet for a picture to colour.

Section 4 Celebrations

- Weddings
- Eid-ul-Fitr
- Chocolate 'celebrations'
- Christmas decorations
- Harvest
- Birthdays
- Presents

Weddings

Needed

A wedding dress, veil, shoes and a bride's bouquet

A buttonhole

A bridesmaid's dress

Wedding invitation, confetti, piece of wedding cake

Wedding rings and engagement ring

Pictures of a wedding

Songs

'I'm getting married in the morning'

The magic penny

'Jesus' love is very wonderful' – JP 139

Talk to the children about weddings and ask if any have been to one.

Show them the dress that the bride might wear. If possible, get one of the children to dress up.

Show them the items that people associate with weddings.

Show them the rings and talk about the special promise that the man and woman say to each other.

If possible, talk about weddings in other faiths, e.g.

In the Jewish faith, the couple stand under a huppa (a canopy).

In the Hindu faith, the bride is dressed in a red sari and has mehndi patterns painted on her hands and feet.

In the Sikh faith, the bride wears a traditional red and gold costume.

Prayer

Thank you, God, for the special celebration of marriage, when two people make a special promise to each other.

Amen

See worksheet for a picture to colour.

Eid-ul-Fitr

Needed

New clothes

Eid cards

Presents

Songs

'When I needed a neighbour' – JP 275

'He's got the whole wide world in his hands' – MP 225

'If you're happy and you know it'

Eid-ul-Fitr is a feast in which Muslims take part at the end of Ramadan.

Everyone bathes and then puts on new clothes. People send Eid cards to their friends. Children receive gifts.

Eid-ul-Fitr is a very special time for people who follow the religion of Islam.

Prayer

Thank you for the special time of Eid. Thank you for good food and good friends.

Amen

See worksheet for pictures to colour.

Chocolate 'celebrations'

Needed

A box of 'Celebration' sweets, or any box that has a variety of sweets, such as liquorice allsorts.

Songs

'This little light of mine' – JP 258

'He's got the whole wide world in his hands' – MP 225

'He gave me eyes so I could see' – JP 74

Bring out your box of sweets and ask who would like one.

Select one each from the assortment of sweets.

Choose some children who can pick out a sweet. Invite the children to choose a sweet and to say what kind it is and why they like that one (or you can describe what they have chosen).

All the sweets are different; yet together they make a complete box. All the children have chosen a different sweet, the one that they like the best.

If everyone liked the same sweet, it would be very difficult. We would not have enough to share around. We would be left with some sweets that no one liked.

All of us are different; yet together we are all people. We are different sizes and different shapes; we have different-coloured skin, hair and eyes. We like some people better than others. We are all needed to make up the world.

Prayer

Thank you for all the people in our school, thank you for all the people in our town, and thank you for all the people in the world.

Amen

See worksheet for pictures to colour and match.

Christmas decorations

Needed

A Christmas tree (or a large picture of one)

Some Christmas decorations (or pictures of them)

Some fairy lights

Songs

'Oh, Christmas tree'

'Away in a manger' – MP 47

'Mary had a baby'

Talk about the things that we put on the tree and the meaning of them.

Angel	The angel Gabriel told Mary she was going to have a baby. An angel told the shepherds that Jesus had been born in the stable.
Star	The three wise men followed a bright star to the stable.
Snowflake	Christmas is celebrated in our wintertime.
Lights	Jesus Christ is the light of the world.
Bells	They ring out to tell people the good news.
Presents	Jesus Christ is our gift from God. The wise men brought gifts for the baby.

Prayer

Thank you, God, for all the lovely things that we see at Christmas time.

Thank you for sending baby Jesus to us.

Amen

See worksheet for decorations to colour.

Harvest

Needed

A variety of fruit and vegetables

A watering can

A washing-up bowl

A picture of the sun

The 'Enormous Turnip' story

Songs

'Thank you, Lord, for this fine day' – JP 232

'I have seen the golden sunshine' – JP 99

'I love the sun'

'What shall we bring for Harvest time?'

Look at each item of fruit in turn and ask the children to name it.

Look at each item of vegetable in turn and ask the children to name it.

What do all these fruit and vegetables need to grow?

They need the sun. They need the rain. (The watering can and washing-up bowl can be used to demonstrate the rain.)

Some need care and attention from a gardener.

Tell the story of the 'Enormous Turnip' and, if possible, get a class to act it out.

Prayer

Dear God, thank you for the sun and the rain, which we need to make things grow. Thank you for all the food that we have to eat.

Amen

See worksheet for fruit and vegetables to colour and sort.

Birthdays

Needed

A birthday cake with candles

Party food to put on the table

Some presents

Balloons and streamers

Songs

'Happy birthday'

'If I were a butterfly' – JP 94

The magic penny

Have an empty table and select some children to put items on it for a party. Discuss what you would need to put out.

Blow up the balloons to decorate the room.

Discuss things you enjoy having and doing for your birthday.

Bring out the birthday cake and put some candles on it. How many candles would you need?

If possible, select a child who is celebrating a birthday to come and blow out the candles.

Cut the cake and let everyone share in the celebration.

Prayer

Thank you, God, for letting us celebrate our birthdays. Thank you for friends and family and for good fun.

Amen

See worksheet for a picture to colour.

Presents

Needed

Some recognizable items – such as a ball, plate, video tape, cassette tape, box of sweets – wrapped up in gift paper

Songs

'Happy birthday'

'If you're happy and you know it'

The magic penny

Talk about having presents.

When do you have presents?

Who gives you presents?

If possible, encourage the children to guess what is in each parcel.

Ask one of them to open each present.

Talk about God sending the special gift of baby Jesus.

Prayer

Thank you for presents that we get for our birthdays and at Christmas.

Thank you for sending us the special gift of baby Jesus.

Amen

See worksheet for pictures to colour and match.

Section 5 Living things

- Chinese New Year
- Valentine's Day
- Mothering Sunday
- Easter
- The story of Noah
- Treasure box
- Water
- Flowers, plants and vegetables

Chinese New Year

Needed

Prawn crackers

Chinese lanterns

Any available Chinese artefacts

A blanket

Songs

'My boat sailed from China'

'He's got the whole wide world in his hands' – MP 225

'Stand up, clap hands' – JP 225

Talk about people from China and how they celebrate their New Year.

The people clean their houses and decorate their living-rooms with vases of blossom. They have plates of oranges and tangerines, and a plate with eight varieties of dried fruit. They hang up happy wishes written in black ink on red paper.

Show the children the Chinese artefacts.

Using a blanket, get a couple of children (or adults) to perform a dragon dance.

The dragon dances around the streets and makes the people happy.

Sample the prawn crackers and other Chinese food.

Prayer

Thank you for our friends from China, as they celebrate their New Year. Please bring them peace and happiness.

Amen

See worksheet for a picture of a Chinese dragon to colour.

Valentine's Day

Needed

A heart-shaped picture

Some Valentine cards

Some flowers and/or chocolates

Songs

The rainbow song

'Jesus' love is very wonderful' – JP 139

The magic penny

Valentine's Day is named after St Valentine of Rome, who died in AD 269. He is believed to have aided Christians who were having a hard time in pagan Rome. It is said that St Valentine was arrested and then killed because he helped Christians to get married during a time when the emperor had forbidden all weddings, because he wanted men for his army and married men were not called up.

The story goes that St Valentine had given children flowers from his garden; so when he was put in prison the children threw flowers to him through the prison bars.

Today, people send cards to each other, but they do not put their name on the card, so it is a secret.

Sometimes you give flowers or chocolates to the person that you love.

Look at some cards.

Prayer

Thank you, God, for all the people that we love. Thank you for St Valentine, who gave the children flowers from his garden.

Amen

See worksheet for hearts to colour.

Mothering Sunday

Needed

A tray set for breakfast

Some flowers

Examples of cards made by the children

Songs

'He's got the whole wide world in his hands' – MP 225

'Jesus' love is very wonderful' – JP 139

The magic penny

Many years ago working girls were allowed to go home to see their mothers only on Mothering Sunday (it falls on the fourth Sunday in Lent). Special cakes would be baked and each working girl would be allowed to take one with her. This was called a 'simnel cake'. It was a rich fruitcake topped with a layer of marzipan and with a layer of marzipan through the middle. Eleven balls of marzipan were put on the top to represent the disciples of Jesus.

Think about all the things your Mum does for you.

What could you do to help her on Mothering Sunday?

What gift could you give her?

Ask the children to show some of the cards they have made.

Prayer

Thank you, God, for our Mums. They are very special and help us to do lots of things. Help us to be good and to help them.

Amen

See worksheet for a picture to colour.

Easter

Needed

Hot cross buns

An Easter egg

A smart hat, or decorated Easter bonnet

Songs

'God's not dead' – JP 60

'I'm special' – JP 106

'We have a king who rides a donkey' – JP 264

Look at a hot cross bun and talk about the cross on the top. This is to remind us that Jesus died on the cross on Good Friday and that he loves us all.

Let everyone have a taste of the hot cross buns.

Share an Easter egg. Talk about the birds that hatch from eggs. Talk about baby animals. The egg is the symbol of new life. Christians believe that God gave us Jesus, who came to life again on Easter Sunday.

Look at the hat, or decorated Easter bonnet. Many years ago people used to have new clothes at Easter. Poor people could not always afford to buy a new set of clothes, but they always tried to get a new hat.

Prayer

Thank you, God, for new life. Thank you for sending your son, Jesus, to be with us.

Amen

See worksheet for a picture of an Easter egg to colour.

The story of Noah

Needed

A Noah bag

(available from Decade Ministries, Tel: 01235 833030)

Some animal pictures, toys or models

A model boat or ark

Songs

'Rise and shine' – JP 210

'Who built the ark?'

'Who put the colours in the rainbow?' – JP 288

Look at all the different animals.

Tell the story of Noah, using the Noah bag.

Talk about making promises and how important it is that we keep our promise.

Prayer

Thank you, God, for your promise to be with us as we live our lives.

Help us to be kind and to help other people and our friends.

Amen

See worksheet for a picture to colour.

Treasure box

Needed

Examples of children's treasure boxes

A jewellery box

A cash box or small safe

Songs

'He gave me eyes so I could see' – JP 74

'Jesus' love is very wonderful' – JP 139

'He's got the whole wide world in his hands' – MP 225

Talk about things that are special and precious.

Where do we keep things that are valuable?

Look at the safe or cash box. We must lock this to make sure that the contents
are safe and secure. Talk about things that we have that are valuable and look at the jewellery
box and its contents.

We all have things that are precious and special for us.

Look at a box that has items which are special for one of the pupils. (Items might include: sweet
wrapper; picture; copy of a favourite video; family photographs; ticket from the pantomime;
objects that remind the pupil of certain people.)

Prayer

Thank you, God, for all the things that are special for us.

Amen

See worksheet for a picture to colour.

Water

Needed

A bottle or jug of water

A bowl

Blue material, or lengths of blue and white ribbon on some sticks

Music to represent water

Songs

'All over the world' – MP 18; JP 5

'Deep and wide' – JP 35

'Thank you, Lord, for this fine day' – JP 232

Think about all the water on the earth. Talk about rivers, seas, lakes, canals, ponds and waterfalls.

We all need water to live. Our bodies are made up of lots of water. We need to drink water every day to keep our bodies healthy.

Ask some children to hold the material (or ribbons on sticks) and wave it (or them) in time to the music. See if they can do this gently, like the sea on a calm day, or fast, like the sea when the weather is stormy.

Arrange the children in a long line, so that the water has become a long river.

Prayer

Thank you, God, for the water that we need to live. Bless all the fish and other creatures that live in the seas and the rivers.

Amen

See worksheet for a picture to colour.

Flowers, plants and vegetables

Needed

A bunch of flowers

Pot plants

Vegetables

Songs

'God, who made the earth' – JP 63

'He's got the whole wide world in his hands' – MP 225

'Who put the colours in the rainbow?' – JP 288

Talk about all the flowers that are growing in the school garden and in gardens at home. Talk about the perfume of the flowers and how pretty they look.

Talk about the plants in the pots. What do they need to be able to grow?

Talk about the vegetables. Where do they grow? What do they need to be able to grow?

We eat vegetables to make us healthy and strong.

Prayer

Thank you, God, for all the flowers that make the world a pretty place to live. Thank you for all the vegetables that we need to make us fit and healthy.

Amen

See worksheet for a picture to colour.

Section 6 Travel

- Transport
- Going on holiday
- Refugees
- Being prepared

Transport

Needed

Pictures or models of a bicycle, a bus, a train, a car, a boat and an aeroplane

Songs

'One more step along the world I go' – JP 188

'Michael, row the boat ashore'

'I have seen the golden sunshine' – JP 99

How did you get to school today? Discuss different kinds of transport. Did you travel in a taxi, on a minibus, or on a big bus?

Talk about the other kinds of transport.

Who has been in a car; a bus; a train; an aeroplane?

Who can ride a bicycle?

All these forms of transport help us to move around much more easily.

When Jesus was a boy there were no cars, trains or aeroplanes; not even bicycles. He had to walk everywhere.

How long would it take to walk to your local town? How long would it take to go shopping? How long would it take to walk to school?

Prayer

Thank you, God, for cars, buses, trains and aeroplanes that make our journeys so much easier. Thank you for being with us on our journeys.

Amen

See worksheet for pictures to colour and match.

Going on holiday

Needed

A suitcase

An assortment of clothes: some suitable for going away on holiday, others not suitable

(Try to include some comical and unusual items.)

Songs

'Thank you, Lord, for this fine day' – JP 232

'I have seen the golden sunshine' – JP 99

'One more step along the world I go' – JP 188

Tell everyone that you are going away on a holiday and need help to pack your case. You need to pack things that you will need for a holiday in the sun.

Pick up one item at a time (or get different children to come out to do this). Decide which items should go in the case.

Should you take wellington boots, or sandals?

Will you need a thick coat, or a bathing costume?

Talk about being ready to go away and being prepared.

Prayer

Dear God, thank you for sunshine and for nice places to visit.
Thank you for opportunities to travel.

Amen

See worksheet for pictures to colour.

Refugees

Needed

A small bag containing essential items

A blanket

A chair and a small table

A purse

Lots of books

Toys and other items

Songs

'When I needed a neighbour' – JP 275

'Give me oil in my lamp' – MP 167

'One more step along the world I go' – JP 188

Remind the children what they need to pack when they are going on a holiday. Talk about the heavy suitcase, with all the things they may need.

What would it be like if you had to leave your home and take all your things with you?

In some countries people have to leave their homes because of war. What would they need to take with them? How could they carry everything?

Choose a child (or an adult) and load them up with many of the items above. Would they be able to travel far?

People who have to flee their homes can only take a few essential things.

Talk about being ready and being prepared.

Prayer

Dear God, bless all the people who have to leave their homes because of problems. Keep them safe in your care.

Amen

See worksheet for a picture to draw and colour.

Being prepared

Needed

Going-out bag

Picnic box

First-aid kit

Songs

'When I needed a neighbour' – JP 275

'One more step along the world I go' – JP 188

'Stand up, clap hands' – JP 225

Who likes going out on visits?

Who likes going out on a picnic?

Do we need to take anything with us when we go?

What would happen if someone had an accident when we were out?

When we go out with school we take our 'going-out' bag, so we are prepared. This contains information sheets, spare nappies, wet wipes, tissues and the mobile phone.

When we go out for a picnic we have all our food and drink in our picnic box.

When we are in the bus or the car we have the first-aid kit, in case someone has an accident.

It is good to be prepared.

Prayer

Dear God, help us to be prepared for whatever happens.

Amen

See worksheet for a game.

Part 2

The worksheets

Introducing the worksheets

Staff at Ysgol y Graig have commented that it is often difficult to find simple worksheets, so that the theme of the assembly can be continued in the classroom. In view of this situation, I have included a collection of activities that can be undertaken as a lead into the worship, or as a follow-up from it.

These worksheets are set at a very simple level. They will reinforce ideas discussed in worship and can easily be adapted and set at an appropriate level for your pupils.

I have included one activity for each assembly. All of these are straightforward and self-explanatory.

Section 1 Light

- Christingle
- Advent
- Hanukkah
- Diwali
- Candles
- Creation
- Traffic lights
- Colours

Christingle

1. The orange is the world

2. The candle is Jesus, light of the world

3. The ribbon is the love of Jesus

4. The cocktail sticks are the four seasons

5. The fruit is the fruit of the earth

Colour the Christingle

Advent

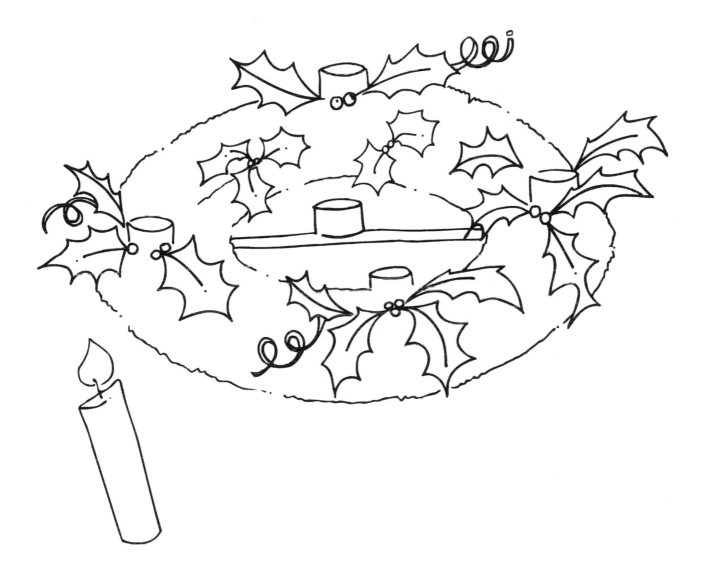

Draw the candles and colour the Advent ring

Hanukkah

The Jewish festival of light

Colour the hanukiah

Diwali

The Hindu festival of light

Colour the floor with rangoli patterns

Candles

Colour and match the candles

Creation

Put some stars in the sky

Put some animals on the earth

Put some fish in the sea

stars   animals   fish

Traffic lights

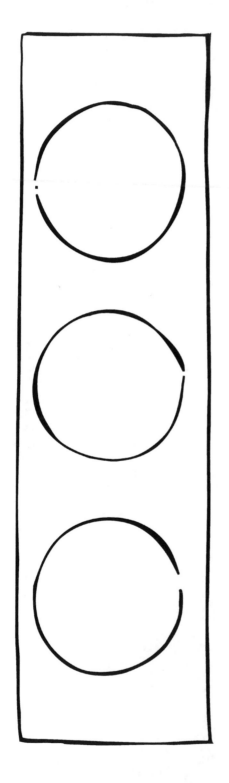 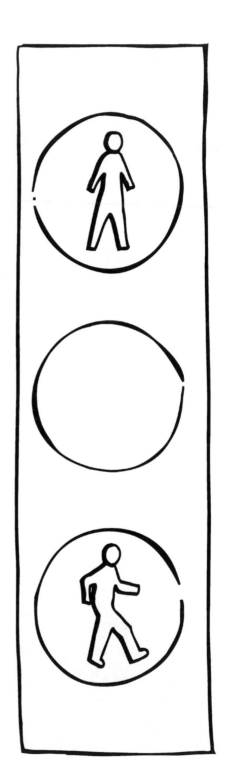

Colour the traffic lights

Colours

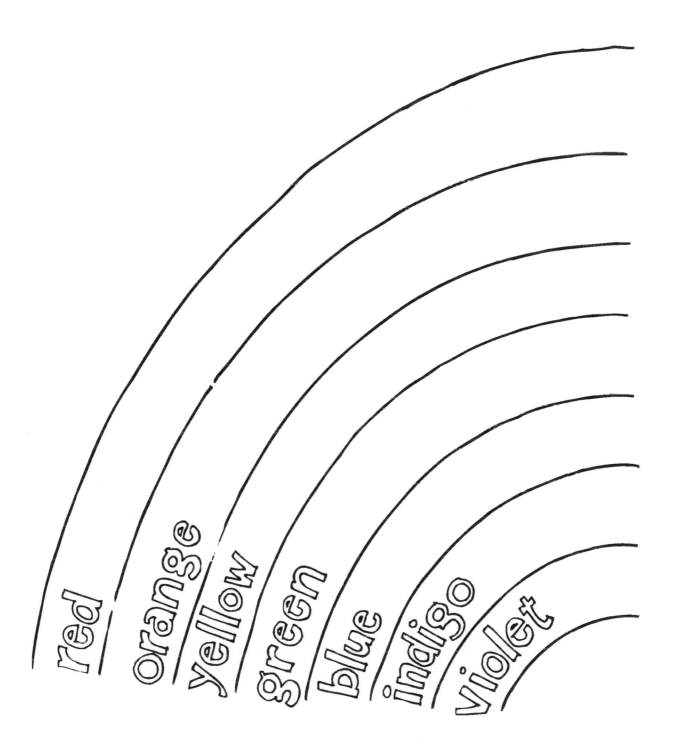

red orange yellow green blue indigo violet

Colour the rainbow

Section 2 Myself

- Hands
- People who help us
- Body parts
- Shoes
- Hats
- Myself
- Baptism

Hands

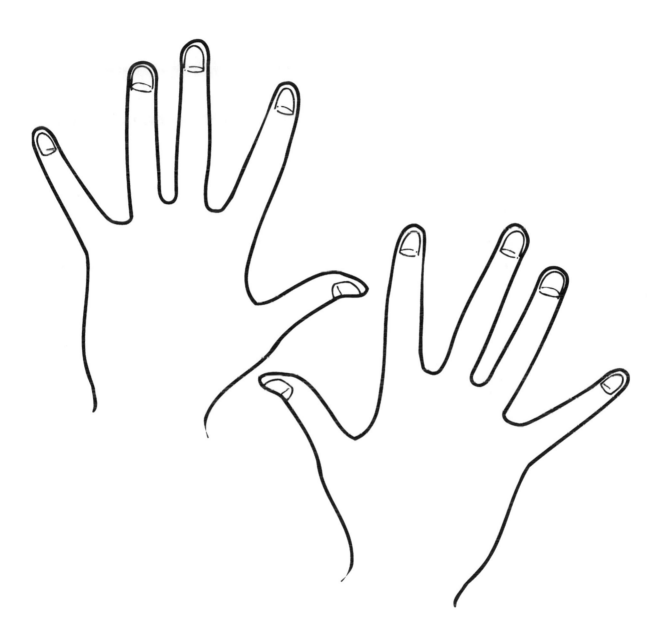

Colour the hands

People who help us

firefighter

ambulance

ambulance worker

police car

police constable

fire engine

Colour the pictures and match each person with a vehicle

Body parts

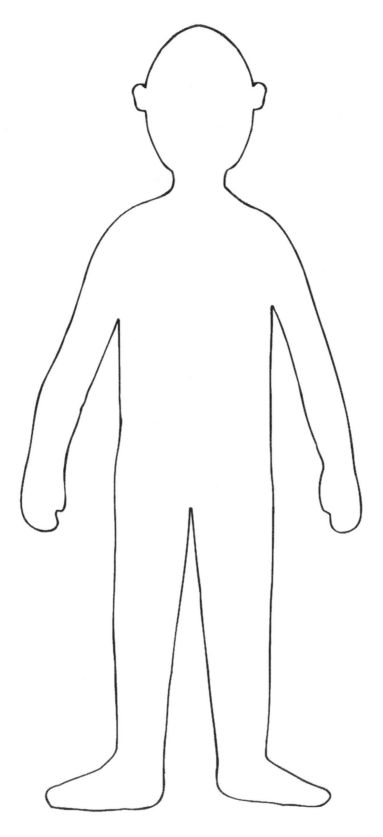

Colour the person to look like you

Shoes
Colour and match

wellington boot

sandal

slipper

slipper

trainer

wellington boot

sandal

trainer

Colour the shoes and then match the pairs

Hats

Who can you see?

Colour the picture

Myself

Who can you see?

Draw a picture of yourself in the mirror

Baptism

A baby is baptized

Colour the picture

Section 3 Homes

- Homes
- Safety in the home
- The environment
- Furniture in the home
- Family life
- Jewish festival of Sukkot
- Animals and their homes
- Homeless

Homes

The wise man built his house upon the rock.

The foolish man built his house upon the sand.

Colour the pictures

Safety in the home

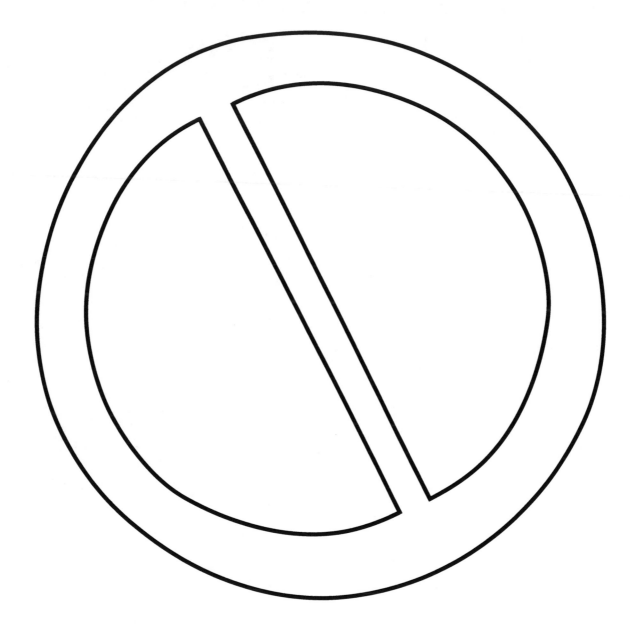

Not available

Colour the picture

The environment

Put a circle around each bottle

Furniture in the home
Goldilocks and the three bears

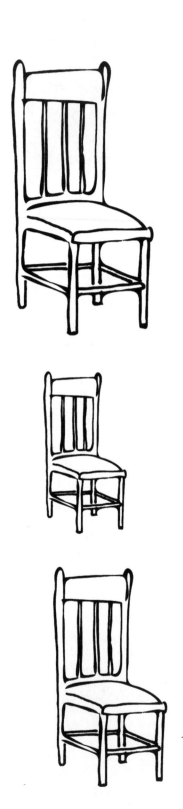

Colour the pictures and match the bears to the chairs

Family life

What can you do to help in the home?

wash the car

wash the dishes

make the bed

set the table

make a cup of tea

Colour the pictures

Jewish festival of Sukkot

Colour the picture

Animals and their homes

dog

rabbit hutch

rabbit

bird cage

bird

basket

Match the animals to their homes and colour the pictures

Homeless

Colour the picture of these people who have no house to live in

Section 4 Celebrations

- Weddings
- Eid-ul-Fitr
- Chocolate 'celebrations'
- Christmas decorations
- Harvest
- Birthdays
- Presents

Weddings
A wedding picture

wedding party

rings

bouquet

wedding cake

Colour the picture

Eid-ul-Fitr

an Eid card

new clothes

presents

Colour the pictures

Chocolate 'celebrations'

Colour and match the sweets

Christmas decorations

present

angels

bells

Stars

snowflakes

light

Colour the decorations

Harvest

Look at the harvest

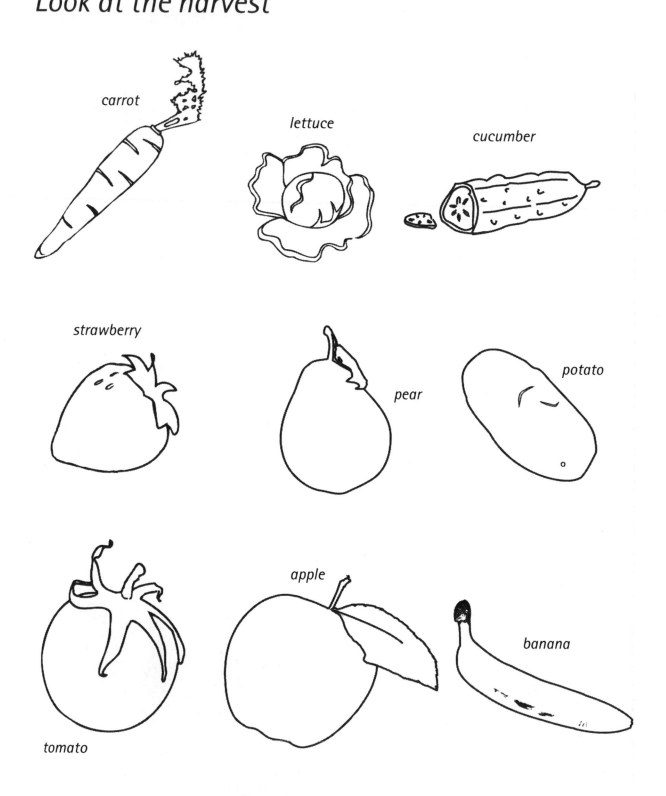

carrot

lettuce

cucumber

strawberry

pear

potato

tomato

apple

banana

Colour the fruit and vegetables
Draw a circle around each fruit

Birthdays

How old are you?

Colour the birthday cake and put some candles on it

Presents

What is in the parcel?

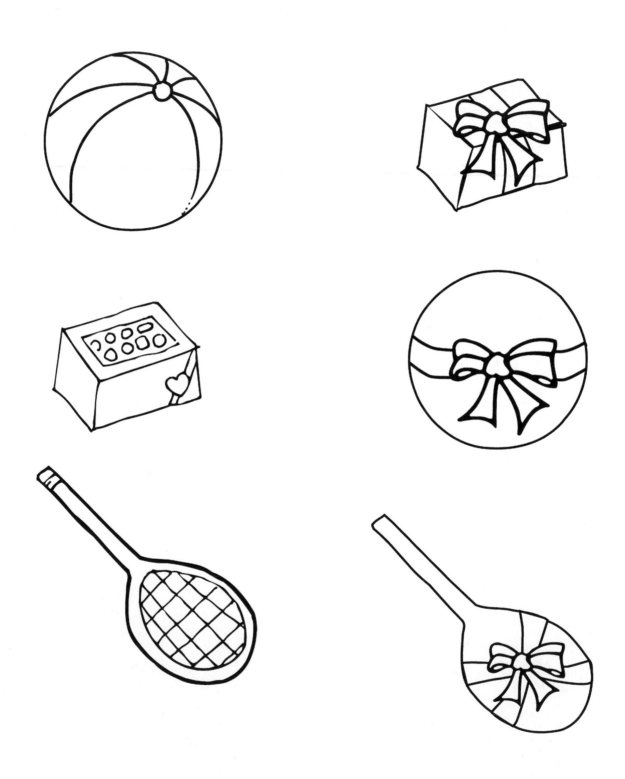

Colour and match the presents

Section 5 Living things

- Chinese New Year
- Valentine's Day
- Mothering Sunday
- Easter
- The story of Noah
- Treasure box
- Water
- Flowers, plants and vegetables

Chinese New Year

Colour the dragon

Valentine's Day

Colour the hearts

Put a circle around the small hearts

Mothering Sunday

Colour and match the presents for Mum

Easter

Colour the Easter egg

The story of Noah

Colour Noah's ark

Treasure box

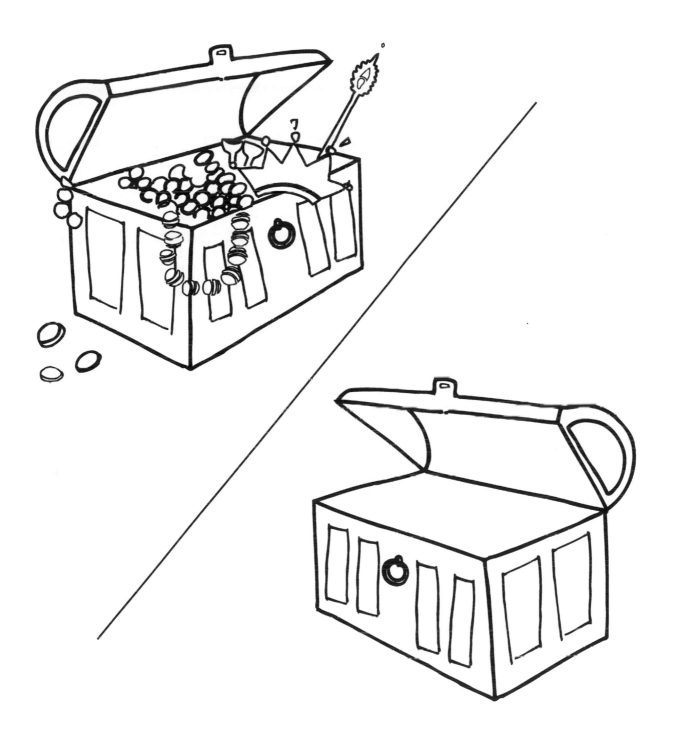

Colour the treasure chest

What will you put in your treasure box?

Water

Colour the picture

Flowers, plants
and vegetables

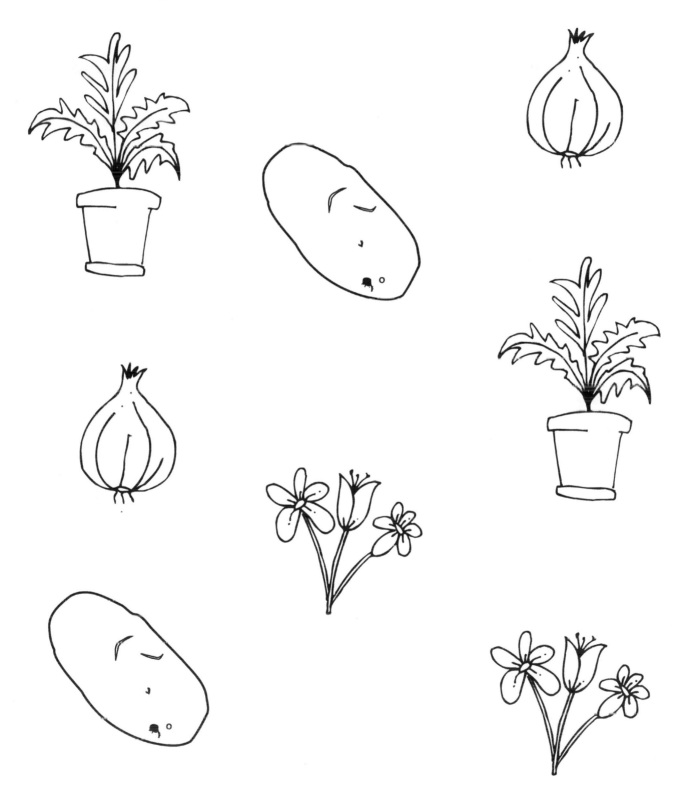

Colour and match

Section 6 Travel

- Transport
- Going on holiday
- Refugees
- Being prepared

Transport

Colour and match the pictures

Going on holiday

What will you pack?

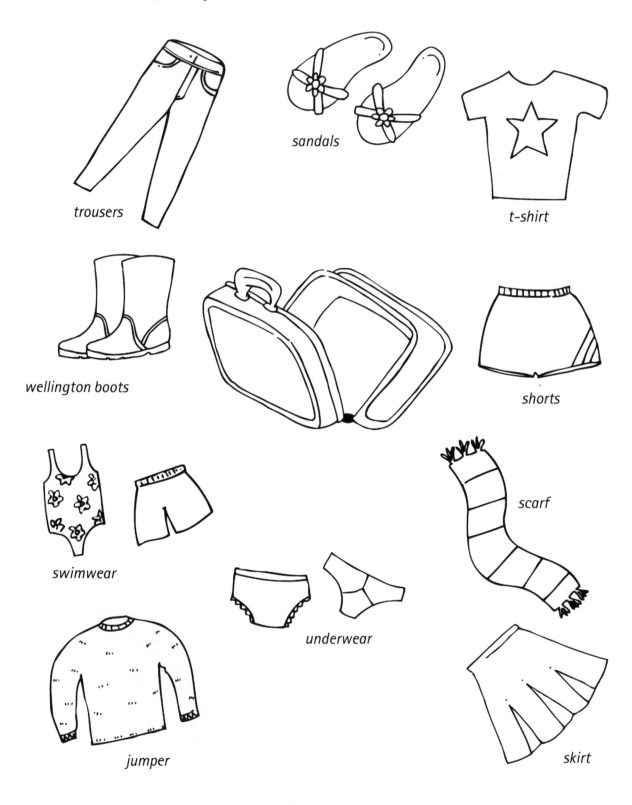

trousers

sandals

t-shirt

wellington boots

shorts

swimwear

scarf

underwear

jumper

skirt

Colour the clothes you will pack in your case

Refugees

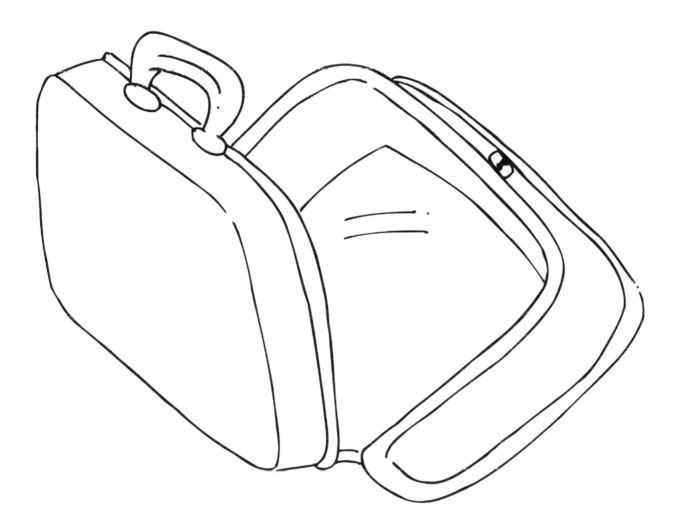

What would you pack?

Being prepared

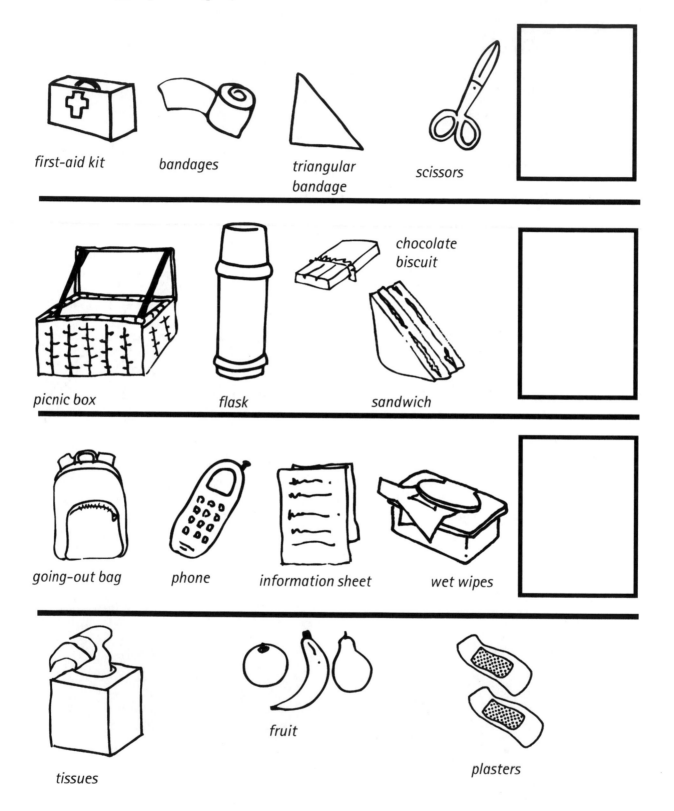

first-aid kit

bandages

triangular bandage

scissors

picnic box

flask

chocolate biscuit

sandwich

going-out bag

phone

information sheet

wet wipes

tissues

fruit

plasters

What is missing? Fill in the missing item

Appendix

- Glossary
- Recipes
- The story of Rama and Sita
- Picture symbols from Rebus and PCS

Glossary

Dreidel game – this is a game played by children of the Jewish faith during Hanukkah. A dreidel is a wooden top that has four sides. The dreidel is spun as a normal top and lands on one of the sides. Each side has the first letter of one of the four Hebrew words making up the sentence 'A great miracle happened there', which are also the first letters of four Yiddish words (a language formerly spoken by Jewish people in Eastern Europe) that give the instructions for the steps in the game. Sweets or matchsticks are placed in the centre, taken out of the centre or shared around, depending on the instruction given by the side on which the dreidel lands.

Menorah – this represents the original seven-branched candelabrum of the Jerusalem temple; it is an important symbol of Judaism.

Hanukiah – this nine-branched candelabrum recalls the miraculous event when one day's supply of oil lasted for eight days, until new supplies came to the temple. An additional candle is lit on each of the eight days, from the (ninth) 'servant' candle that is placed in a raised holder in the middle. See also the act of worship 'Hanukkah'.

Diva lamps – these are small saucer-shaped clay lamps that are painted and highly decorated. Their wicks were originally made out of twisted cotton, which was dipped in melted butter. They were lit to guide Rama, Sita and Lakshmana back to Ayodhya after their 14 years of exile. Today, diva lamps are filled with small night lights.

Mehndi – at Hindu weddings members of the bride's family decorate her hands and feet with intricate patterns, which are usually in geometric or floral designs. Muslim women also use them on special occasions, such as festival times.

Rangoli patterns – these are patterns that are drawn on the floor of the entrance of each house. Some Hindus draw them daily as a way of welcoming guests. They are made with the fingers, using grains of rice, flour or coloured chalks. The patterns are usually circles, squares and rectangles, but always follow a geometric design.

Recipes

Latkes

4 medium-sized potatoes

1 medium-sized onion, grated

4 tablespoonfuls self-raising flour

2 eggs, lightly beaten

Salt and pepper

Oil for frying

Method

Wash, peel and grate the potatoes and drain well (squeeze, to get rid of as much moisture as possible). Mix with the grated onion, flour, eggs, salt and pepper. Fry tablespoonfuls of the mixture in a little oil until golden brown; then turn over and brown the other side.

Sweets for Diwali

225g desiccated coconut

100g icing sugar, plus some for coating the sweets

200g condensed milk

Food colouring *(optional)*

Method

Mix all the ingredients together. Roll the mixture into walnut-sized balls and coat with icing sugar. Put aside to set.

The story of Rama and Sita

A long time ago, in India, there was a king called Dasharatha [Da-sha-ra-tha] who ruled over the kingdom of Ayodhya. The king had three wives and three sons. The eldest son was called Prince Rama. He was handsome and very clever.

King Dasharatha said it was time for Rama to get married. At length, Rama chose a wife called Sita. Rama and Sita got married and were very happy.

Rama knew that he was to be king after his father died. But one of Rama's stepmothers wanted her son to be king, so she asked King Dasharatha to send Rama to the forest for 14 years.

Sita was a loyal wife and went to live in the forest with Prince Rama. Lakshmana, who was one of Rama's half-brothers, went to the forest with them. They all lived together and were very happy. They also learned many things from the holy men who were living in the forest.

Rama and Lakshmana went out hunting to get meat for them to eat. When they left home, Rama put a magic circle around the house to make sure that Sita would be safe while they were away.

One day, when Rama and Lakshmana were out, a demon king called Ravanna changed himself into a golden deer and tricked Sita into leaving her safe circle. He kidnapped her and took her away to the island of Sri Lanka.

As she was being taken away, Sita left behind her a trail of jewellery. Rama and Lakshmana followed this trail. They had many adventures on their way to find her. They met a monkey called Hanuman, and he and a group of his monkey friends lay down to make themselves into a bridge over the sea to the island of Sri Lanka.

After ten years of fighting, Rama finally killed the demon Ravanna and rescued Sita.

When they heard the news that Rama's father had died, Rama, Sita and Lakshmana set out for home. The people of Ayodhya heard that they were coming back and lit lots of tiny lights and made bright decorations to show them the way home.

Rama, Sita and Lakshmana, and all the people, were very pleased that Rama would be crowned king at last. He would rule the people in a fair and proper way.

Every year, Hindu people light little candles and decorate their homes to celebrate Diwali and to remember the story of Rama and Sita.

Picture symbols from Rebus and PCS

Sing

Prayer

Story

Holiday

Special mention

Bibliography

Government publications

Education Reform Act 1988

Religious Education and Collective Worship Circular 1/94

Resources

Published materials

E. Breuilly and S. Palmer, *A Tapestry of Tales*, Collins Educational, 1993.

L. J. Francis and N. M. Slee, *Neighbours*, National Christian Education Council, 1990.

L. J. Francis and N. M. Slee, *The Broken Leg*, National Christian Education Council, 2001.

Peter Horrobin and Greg Leavers (compilers), *Junior Praise*, Marshall Pickering, 1986.

Peter Horrobin and Greg Leavers (compilers), *Mission Praise*, Marshall Pickering, 1999.

S. Murrell, *Faith in a Box*, Farmington Institute web site: www.farmington.ac.uk, 2001.

Captain A. Price, *Kidsource*, Kevin Mayhew Ltd, 1999.

V. Voiles, *Hinduism: A new approach*, London, 1998.

Divali: A resource pack, The Multicultural and Equal Opportunities Centre, Newcastle-upon-Tyne.

Suppliers

Religious artefacts and resources for education can be purchased from:

Articles of Faith Ltd, Resources House, Kay Street, Bury BL9 6BU. Tel: 0161 763 6232; web site: www.articlesoffaith.co.uk

Religion in Evidence, TTS, Monk Road, Alfreton, Derbyshire, DE55 7RL. Tel: 0800 318686; web site: www.tts-group.co.uk